CORNV

SINCE 1900

100 Years of Photographs

1. The Village Fair at Boscastle, from a 1905 postcard. Boscastle Fair was quite an event in this area of North Cornwall, and was the subject of a song my old friend, the late Charlie Jose, used to sing. The song began: "I went down to Boscastle Fair, and I purchased a nice pen of lambs, but when I got home and sorted 'em out I found that the blinkers was rams. I'm a most unfortunate chap, did you ever hear tell such a case, Nort nothing goes right from morning till night, 'tis enough to drive anyone maze." RIC Photo, Boscastle 38.

First published 1990

Archive Publications Ltd
10 Seymour Court
Manor Park
RUNCORN
Cheshire

in association with

Western Morning News
Leicester Harmsworth House
65 New George Street
PLYMOUTH

ISBN 0 948946 80 6

Contents

Introduction

As we entered the 1990s, and in the first few months there was so much change in the world, I thought it would be interesting to collect together some photographs which would show Cornwall over the past 100 years.

This is not a history book, just a nostalgic look back to the turn of the century and also to Cornwall since the war. By using old photographs of those days before the motor car and then, in some instances, adding a picture of the same scene today I have tried to show how places have changed.

As I began to explore the collection of the Royal Institution of Cornwall at the County Museum in Truro and the more modern files of *The Western Morning News* I found threads which would link the early pictures to the present day. First there was the Great Blizzard of January 1891, which saw snow on the ground from March until June, and the terrible storms of January 1990, which wrecked some of Cornwall's sea defences, damaged houses and buildings including Truro Cathedral, and laid waste thousands of beautiful trees and gardens.

The book could have been titled "Cornwall — from Blizzard to Storm" but it is not my intention to stick to a weather theme. However, those two catastrophic events 99 years apart show us that we are still at the mercy of the elements now, just as people were before the 20th century had even started.

Another thread which ran throughout the files that I examined was the presence of pictures of so many Royal visits to Cornwall. As a journalist in Cornwall it has been my pleasure to report on many of the visits by members of the Royal family to the county, including our own Duke and Duchess of Cornwall. So the pictures in this book also run from the Prince of Wales in 1905 at Falmouth to the Princess of Wales, Duchess of Cornwall, in Truro in 1990. These are simply glimpses at our county yesterday and today, plus some occasions which I have attended and found interesting. I hope you enjoy them too.

Many people have helped me to collect the pictures and material for this book, especially Roger Penhallurick, of the Royal Institution of Cornwall, whose enthusiasm and knowledge meant that I was soon able to locate items I wanted from their files. Photographs reproduced by kind permission of the Royal Institution of Cornwall are marked RIC and usually carry a number for easy location if copies are required.

Ken Doble, former deputy editor of *The Western Morning News*, located some of the old picture files, while others I should thank include chief photographer John Chapman, printer Tim Wellam, and freelance photographers David Brenchley, Colin Higgs and John Lyne, all of whom have work reproduced here. Many early pictures were reproduced as postcards and some of those used here were loaned by David Taylor, who has one of the largest collections in Cornwall on sale at his shop Carousel, Fore Street, St Ives.

2. Colin Gregory.

Colin Gregory is a Cornishman who has worked for *The Western Morning News* since 1972. In the Plymouth Head Office he was picture editor and deputy chief sub-editor, while in Cornwall he has been the district chief reporter, based at Truro.

He was a pupil at Launceston College and then entered journalism with the *Cornish and Devon Post* at Launceston before continuing his education at Cornwall Technical College and Bristol Polytechnic, after which he worked as an accountant and in industry before returning to newspapers.

He enjoys reporting on the ups and downs of life in Cornwall, a place which is never dull and is full of characters. From covering a council meeting to sitting in the crowded stand at a county rugby match, from reporting a small case at the Magistrate's Court to being involved in the coverage of a major murder inquiry, he says life as a journalist in Cornwall is never lacking in variety.

His interests outside journalism are travel, especially in France, and building up his extensive collection of antique toys.

3. Miners waiting to descend the pit near Redruth, which at various times has been the centre of world tin production. This postcard of an original black and white photograph was coloured and printed in Germany for sale in Cornwall.

Cornwall at the Turn of the Century

The first photograph known to exist in this country was taken in the Westcountry by Henry Fox Talbot at Lacock in Wiltshire in 1835, and from that day a new means of chronicling the everyday life of people and places was born.

Six years later Fox Talbot came to Cornwall to visit Sir Charles Lemon, his uncle by marriage, who lived at Carclew. It was on this visit in 1841 that he made a number of family images which were later published as the first Cornish photographs.

A picture taken by Robert Hunt of the view from his home in Falmouth may have been earlier by a few weeks, but, whoever was the first, photography had come to Cornwall and through its medium we have been able to observe the rapid changes in society.

Experiments in photography had been taking place in Cornwall since 1839, and eventually each town had its photographer, usually a watch or clockmaker or the owner of a general store looking for a new sideline, who took likenesses and recorded local events.

By the 1990s, when this book takes up the story, there were many fine practitioners and they took their cameras down mines, up on cliffs and out in all sorts of weather to get their pictures.

As this publication is linked with *The Western Morning News* I have searched through the files for pictures of events the newspaper has covered or people who have been in the news.

There is a shortage of pictures during the years leading up to the last war, and the blame for that can be laid on the shoulders of one man: Adolf Hitler.

The German airforce laid siege to Plymouth in no uncertain way during the years of the Blitz, 1940-41. One of the bombs hit a firewatchers' shelter near *The Western Morning News* building, Harmsworth House, in New George Street, Plymouth, and the blaze spread to the photographic department. As well as wrecking Sir Harold Harmsworth's Rolls Royce it also damaged our collection of glass plates. I have spoken to people working in our Plymouth office at the time and it is generally believed that the whole stock, even those that were not damaged, were removed and not seen again.

However, there is a good selection of wartime pictures after that date, some showing bomb damage but most of them illustrating the fighting spirit of those left in Cornwall, mainly women and children, who, as picture 103 shows, were determined to put another nail in Hitler's coffin.

I have also taken the opportunity to use extracts from the Cornwall Police war diaries to illustrate that, although not as badly hit as the industrial cities, Cornwall certainly knew there was a war going on.

With few *Western Morning News* photographs available from pre-1940 I was fortunate to have the assistance of the curator of the Royal Institution of Cornwall, Roger Penhallurick, in helping me to search through their wonderful collection for some early pictures.

4. Newquay Harbour. With its fishing boats and small coasters this is a scene which has not changed dramatically today. However, the town behind has expanded to become one of the country's premier resorts.

As, in the 1990s, we become more aware of the fragility of our planet and the rapidly increasing damage being done to it, we also look to the past to see how they lived. Less hurry, less comfort, but when it comes to the burning question of survival, they could show us a thing or two in doing less damage, of living a more natural life and letting nature take its course.

To that bit of home-spun philosophy must be added the fact that times were hard, almost cruel, and if one really had to make the choice between living in the 1890s and the 1990s the decision would be to go for a micro-waved hamburger and a job in a warm office rather than going down one of those cold, wet and dangerous mines with a pasty for lunch.

Journalists observe human life, preferably the more interesting aspects, so this is not a highly researched history book but a few stabs with a hat pin at pictures, events and times I have found interesting. There are many other avenues to be explored if the opportunity arises, especially if the plates of those wonderful early photographs used in *The Western Morning News* between 1900 and 1940 ever come to light.

Cornwall 1890 to 1990 can only start at one point, a browse through *The Western Morning News* as that exciting period began 100 years ago. I turned the page to January 1st, 1890, and although things were so much different then, and the reporting was carried out in a style we would hardly recognise, there are many links with the present day.

The edition which heralded in the 1890s had advertisements on the front page. Spooners, a name not that far distant in Plymouth's commercial scene, were holding their winter sale. The Great Western Railway was advertising trips to Guernsey and Jersey, using fast trains and their ferries.

The style of reporting then was much different from today, with full transcripts of the meetings of bodies which would only rate a paragraph or two today. However, it was accurate, fair and interesting to the people in Cornwall at that time, a philosophy we hope we still maintain.

Mining Intelligence was a popular column, carrying a list of 23 quoted shares in companies such as Blue Hills, Cook's Kitchen, South Crofty and Wheal Kitty. The column reported that shareholders in Carn Brea Mine received a dividend of £1 per share. A breakdown of the accounts showed that total labour costs were £10,400, sales totalled £22,618 and there was a total profit of £9,746.

A report which tells how long the idea of travelling beneath the sea to France has been mooted was also in that January edition in 1890. The Channel Tunnel Company had held a meeting where the engineer reported that works had already been carried out in the tunnel for 2,200 yards. The chairman said the company had proved "beyond doubt that a tunnel could be made easily, cheaply and in a comparatively short space of time." The company had also seen designs of a bridge across the channel, but thought it would mean too many piers and obstructions to shipping.

5. The Old Mill and the Wellington Hotel at Boscastle. The buildings have hardly changed, and the remains of the mill wheel are still in position in this North Cornwall harbour. However, you will not see many cattle or ponies and traps in the street these days.

6. *Stuck in the Blizzard. This Great Western Railways broad gauge 4-4-0 Leopard was derailed at Stray Park, Camborne, during the Great Blizzard of March 9th, 1891. RIC Photo, Locos 10.*

That report of the Channel Tunnel Company could almost have come from the past few years, but an indication of the times came in two other reports from January 1890.

At Wheal Agar Mine 30 female labourers were paid between 2d (one new pence) and 8d (four new pence) per day. A photograph of those hardy mining women, or Bal Maidens, appears in chapter five. The American West was also still wild. There is a report of a man from Iowa and his three children being scalped by Redskins.

It was a hard life for the working man and woman in Cornwall, but when you see photographs of them you can see they had plenty of spirit and pride.

There were similarities between the 1890s and 1990s in Cornwall. The county was the most important metal mining region in the United Kingdom, but by the mid-1890s production had changed dramatically.

In the 1840s Cornwall was producing a wide range of minerals, but 50 years later copper production had slumped from £1million to just £10,000. In 1890 tin production was buoyant but in the middle of the decade difficulties in the tin market caused prices to slump by nearly a third and output was suddenly halved. History seems to be repeating itself in the 1990s. However, to put the position in perspective it must be pointed out that in 1897 there were 31 working tin mines, albeit less than half the number of four years before. If history does repeat itself then there is hope for the present tin industry, because by 1900 prices had doubled from the low levels of five years before.

Soon after that time mining operations had been abandoned in most of the once famous mining districts except those around Carn Brea and at Levant, St Just, and the small operations at West Kitty and Wheal Kitty, St Agnes.

Thousands of Cornishmen had left or were leaving for the mines of America and Australia, agriculture was depressed, but the china clay industry was developing in mid-Cornwall and quarries were busy producing granite and slate.

The potential of tourism was being grasped and hotels were springing up in our main seaside towns, from Penzance up to Bude.

It was the development of tourism which almost certainly gave Cornwall's photographers of those days a boost because they were able to sell their pictures of local scenes as postcards, some of which are reproduced in this volume.

7. ***above:*** *Rosewarne House at Camborne after the Great Blizzard. Notice the two little boys in front of the house amongst the snow and fallen trees. RIC Photo, Camborne 104.*

8. ***below:*** *The Bay of Panama with jute from Calcutta was caught in the Great Blizzard and wrecked at Nare Point, St Anthony-in-Meneage, on March 10th, 1891. RIC Photo.*

9. Penzance around 1890.

Many Cornish people have never really come to terms with tourism. They were used to making their living battling with the elements by mining, fishing or farming. Catering for holidaymakers has always been seen as something the wife might do for pin-money, not a "real" job, and hence the developments in the tourism industry, from hotels to leisure parks, have been carried out by people from outside who have come to Cornwall with a fresh eye, seen the potential and made the most of it.

We seem to enjoy fighting against the odds, be it making a living from the sea, when the powers-that-be put every obstacle in the way of the small fisherman, to watching our boys on the rugby field playing against counties that have a wealth of top players from the fashionable clubs to choose from.

Life has changed in Cornwall as it has everywhere else, but there is still an independence of spirit. Even the people who come down here to live often do so because they want to pursue the sort of life they want to live rather than the one which was dictated to them by living in a city.

Leaving my personal thoughts that the Cornish are different, let us just look at how life has changed in the 100 years between our first photographs and those that have been taken in 1990.

A lot of the beauty of the countryside and coastline has been destroyed, but, thankfully, a lot of it remains. Industrial development, such as the mines, bridges and viaducts built in the last century, are now things to be cherished. I would be very surprised if much of the development today emerged in the same favourable light in 100 years' time, so we have to ensure that any new building in sensitive areas should be to a high standard.

Some of the pictures show the changes in life in Cornwall far better than ever I could in words. Just look at the people in picture 44, could they have imagined that just a few miles from where they were pictured an aeroplane would have been flying to the Scillies less than 50 years later.

Then think about those about to take off in that de Havilland Dragon in 1937. Would they ever have imagined that their children could fly to New York on Concorde in less time than it took them to get to the Scillies and have lunch.

Travel has probably been the biggest change to Cornwall. The motor car has brought tourists to the county in numbers our grandparents would never have imagined. The distance has also worked against some of the county's industry. Industrialists have centralised their production on bases near to the European Market.

However, the way communications are developing it may be no more difficult to base high-tec industries and those concerned with design, printing and information in Cornwall than anywhere else.

Whatever happens, let us hope that Cornwall stays different.

Watch a fishing boat chugging back to port on the high tide, walk on moors or cliffs and imagine the hard graft that went on below those engine houses, find those little pubs in country villages and harbours where people sing those Cornish songs, there is nowhere quite like it.

10. **above:** *Penzance a few years later and more houses have been built, but the harbour area has changed little.*

11. **below:** *Castle Beach at Falmouth, around 1890, with the Falmouth Hotel looming above.*

12. ***above:*** *Launceston High Street from the Square, or Broad Street, around 1900. RIC Photo, Launceston 5.*

13. ***below:*** *Launceston, 1990. Virtually a century on and this scene has not changed above shop front level. Note the guttering which still looks in need of adjustment. I broadened the angle for this shot to show the old granite windows.*

14. **above:** *The Torpoint Ferry from a postcard sent in May, 1907. RIC Photo, Antony 1.*

15. **above:** *The view down Molesworth Street, Wadebridge, in 1909. RIC Photo, Wadebridge 6.*

16. **above:** *The same view today. Telephone lines and cars are the main difference.*

17. Market Jew Street at Penzance in its Victorian splendour.

18. **above:** *The Promenade at Penzance.*

19. **below: T***he Promenade at Penzance from the Western end.*

20. ***above:*** *Gas Court, a back street off Market Jew Street at Penzance.*

21. ***below:*** *Everybody loved the fair. A large crowd outside the Hawkins Arms at Zelah, said to be on their way to Summercourt Fair. RIC Photo, St Alen 6.*

22. *St Austell's Fore Street in 1890.*

23. ***above:*** *Another Fore Street. This time it is Bodmin, and that child would not be standing in the middle of this busy street in 1990. RIC Photo, Bodmin 1.*

24. ***above:*** *Further down Fore Street, Bodmin.*

25. ***above:*** *Looking down Redruth Fore Street.*

26. ***above:*** *Camborne. Looking into Church Street from College Street, a photograph by J C Burrow around 1900. RIC Photo, Camborne 130.*

27. ***below:*** *The same scene by the author, 1990. Note that an extra two storeys have been added to the building on the right.*

28. ***above:*** *At the other end of Camborne we have a dozen fine horses transporting the 40-ton "bob" for the 80-inch pumping engine for Wheal Grenville Mine from Holman Bros in 1906. RIC Photo, Camborne 66.*

29. ***below:*** *March, 1990, and the stone-fronted No 1 machine shop and foundry have been demolished to make way for a supermarket.*

30. **above:** *The old timber viaduct which used to carry the railway over Falmouth Road, Redruth.*

31. **above:** *Churchtown, St Agnes, in the early 1900s. RIC Photo, St Agnes RS/C 9.*

32. **above:** *St Agnes Brass Band in 1914. RIC Photo, St Agnes P1.*

33. **above:** *Liskeard Fore Street in 1906.*

34. **above:** *The same scene in 1987, with some of the original buildings remaining.*

35. ***above:*** *Christmas puddings at St Austell. There was no caption in our files for this picture but it appears to show hospital staff.*

36. ***above:*** *A peaceful scene around the old bridge at Lostwithiel from a Frith and Co postcard of the early 1900s.*

37. ***below:*** *How The Western Morning News reported the untimely demise of the Red Lion.*

LORRY CAREERS INTO HOTEL

Hero driver stayed at wheel

A heavy laden lorry careered out of control through the crowded streets of Truro yesterday morning, and ploughed into the front of the historic Red Lion Hotel, in the city centre.

All guests staying at the Red Lion were last night transferred to the Royal Hotel in Lemon Street, as surveyors said that part of the Red Lion is unsafe.

The crash occurred at 11.15 am, when both pedestrian and vehicular traffic were particularly heavy — but the only person injured was the driver, 41-year-old West Indian Mr Claude Gourzong, a married man from Megavissey.

Hundreds of people watched as firemen fought for two hours to release him from the cab of his lorry, where he was trapped by his left leg.

When released, Mr Gourzong was rushed to the Royal Cornwall Hospital, where it was stated last night that he had a severely fractured left leg.

"His condition is very good," a spokesman said after Mr Gourzong had returned from the operating theatre.

The action of Mr Gourzong in staying at the controls instead of leaping to safety was described afterwards by Chief Supt S.K. Keast as "most heroic."

He said: "If he had left his cab a number of people might easily have been mown down and killed as the streets were full of shoppers at the time."

The lorry went out of control at the top of steep Lemon Street. As it careered towards the city centre, with its headlights on and horn blaring, Mr Gourzong leaned from the cab shouting "My brakes have failed."

38. **above:** *A wonderful sight in Truro in the early 1900s. The Royal Hotel carriage, with the Probus horse-bus behind, outside the Red Lion Hotel in Boscawen Street. The Red Lion was demolished by a runaway lorry in 1967. RIC Photo, BS106.*

39. **below:** *The same scene today, with a supermarket in place of the Red Lion.*

40. **above:** *The Mill, by the Bridge at Boscastle. A Herbert Hughes photograph in 1905. RIC Photo, Boscastle 23.*

41. **below:** *Children playing leapfrog on the Banjo Pier at Looe in 1904. Note the photographers with their large cameras on tripods who have been included in this scene by Herbert Hughes. RIC Photo, Looe 23.*

Transport and Travel

42. **above:** *The horse ferry at King Harry Passage on the River Fal, 1908. The ferry, which crosses from a spot near Trelissick and saves the traveller to The Roseland a lengthy journey by road, now carries cars but is still a magical crossing, especially when big ocean-going ships are laid up either side.*

43. **below:** *The ferry 20 years later.*

44. **above:** *Off to town. The way most country families travelled at the turn of the century. Photo by S and J Govier, believed to be in the St Buryan area. RIC Photo, St Buryan 11.*

45. **below:** *The Helston-Cury-Mullion horse-bus Fairy in the early 1900s, probably outside the Angel Hotel. RIC Photo, Helston 31.*

46. **above:** *What a difference 40 years make. Channel Air Ferries start their flights to the Isles of Scilly from St-Just-in-Penwith in September, 1937, with eight-seater de Havilland Dragons. There was one flight per day in each direction, £1 single, 35/- return.*

47. **above:** *Men at work, or rather having a break to record their work on film. This postcard by Fred J Paul, Calstock, shows work in progress on the viaduct to the village.*

48. **above:** *The first train across the viaduct at Calstock on March 2nd, 1908. The men in the previous picture certainly did their work well. RIC Photo, Railways, Calstock Viaduct 18.*

49. ***above:*** *The Camborne and Redruth Tramway. Car No 6, one of two single-deck California type cars seen on trial at Pool, between the two towns. RIC Photo, Camborne-Redruth Tramway 2.*

50. ***below:*** *Another tram, this time with an upper deck and advertisements for local firms including the Redruth Brewery.*

51. The Lively of Bideford unloading coal alongside the quay at Boscastle, probably in 1905. RIC Photo, Boscastle 15.

52. **above:** *Truro Railway Station, showing the Bulldog class locomotive Tasmania built in 1904 and numbered 3457. The picture was taken before 1912 when the engine was renumbered 3395. RIC Photo, Truro Railway Station 5.*

53. **above:** *Newsagents stand on the platform at Truro Station during the First World War, with headlines proclaiming "Trade Unions Fooled by Politicians" and "Admiral Jellicoe's Farewell to Lord Kitchener." RIC Photo, Truro Railway Station 8.*

54. ***above:*** *The old West Cornwall railway station at Newham, Truro, in the early 1900s when it was a Great Western Railway goods depot. RIC Photo, Truro Railway Station 17.*

55. ***above:*** *One of the railway buildings at Newham, still standing in 1990 and now converted into offices for a bank.*

56. ***above:*** *Goonbell viaduct, near St Agnes, on the old Newquay to Chacewater branch line, under construction in 1902. RIC Photo, Goonbell Viaduct 1.*

57. ***above:*** *Coach and four outside the Falcon Hotel at Bude around 1910. RIC Photo, Bude 47.*

58. ***below:*** *Truro's last steam train in May, 1964.*

59. **above:** *The closure of St Agnes station on February 4th, 1963.*

60 & 61. **above and below:** *Helston's last passenger train on November 5th, 1962.*

62. **above:** *Collegewood Viaduct at Penryn on the Falmouth to Truro branch line. Brunel's timber structure being replaced by concrete in 1934. RIC Photo, Collegewood Viaduct 3.*

63. **below:** *The Uganda leaves the Fal in 1986. This popular cruising ship had been laid up in the river, above the King Harry Ferry, after service in the Falklands. The aerial view by David Brenchley, of Cornish Photonews, shows Trelissick in the background.*

Emergencies on Land and Sea

64. The huge battleship Warspite, 30,000 tons, went aground on a ledge of rocks in Prussia Cove in 1947 while on her way to the breaker's yard. She had broken clear of her tugs in a storm and was eventually turned into scrap on Marazion beach.

65. **above:** *The liner SS Paris was wrecked at Lowland Point, St Keverne, May 21st, 1899. She became a local attraction, and sightseers were ferried out for a closer look. RIC Photo.*

66. **above:** *The SS Rosedale, of London, was wrecked on Portminster Beach, St Ives, during the Cintra gale of November 17th, 1893. Behind is the lifeboat Reserve No 7 which made an unsuccessful attempt to reach her. RIC Photo.*

67. **below:** *The RNLI Edith, the Mullion lifeboat at Mullion Cove in the early 1890s. RIC Photo, RNLI Edith 2.*

68. **above:** *The Padstow lifeboat Edmund Harvey on her inauguration day in 1901. Behind is the tug Helen Peele.*

70. **below:** *An RAF Wessex rescue helicopter arrived to assist with rescue operations. The two photographs illustrate a remarkable rescue.*

69. **above, left:** *The French trawler Jeanne Gougy, wrecked off Land's End in November, 1962. Almost unbelievably six crew members were snatched from certain death when the vessel ran onto the rocks. At first it was believed all the crew had been lost, but shortly before mid-day one of the crowd on the cliff-top saw movement in the wheelhouse. A rocket line was fired and the long slow rescue procedure commenced.*

71. ***above:*** *The plight of the freighter Flying Enterprise floating helplessly off the Cornish coast in January 1952 had the world enthralled. Her captain, Kurt Carlsen, refused to leave his ship while there was any chance of saving her. He was later joined on board for the final hours by Ken Dancey, the mate of the tug Turmoil, who jumped on to the Flying Enterprise. Both men would not leave until the tow parted and the freighter rolled on her side, when they leapt into the sea to be rescued. Only Captain Carlsen knew his ship was carrying components for America's first nuclear submarine, a secret he kept for the rest of his life at sea. He died in 1989, aged 75.*

72. ***below:*** *The Warspite again, with her high turrets but no guns off Prussia Cove in 1947.*

73 & 74. **above and below:** *Cars come to grief as well. I like the look of the breakdown lorry that attended this collision between a Ford and a Standard Vanguard at Perranarworthal in 1951.*

75. ***above:*** *Heavy seas breaking over the coaster Alacrity, grounded near Pendeen in September, 1963. She proved a problem for many years because pieces of her metal, honed razor sharp by time and tide, stuck out of the sand and cut the feet of holidaymakers.*

76. ***above:*** *The British tanker Hemsley (1,178 tons) aground on the North Cornwall coast near Padstow in May, 1969. Built in 1916, she was the oldest ship in the Merchant Navy.*

77. ***above:*** *Thankfully some accidents almost have an air of comedy about them. These potatoes, pictured by John Lyne of Launceston, took to the road when the lorry carrying them overturned on the A30 near Lewannick. It was a backbreaking task for the potato pickers.*

78. The three-masted schooner La Dame du Serk aground at St Mawes in February, 1986. She was, happily, refloated. Picture by Colin Higgs.

79. **above:** *St Austell Fire Brigade on an early Merryweather engine around the turn of the century. What a fine looking body of men. RIC photo, FB2.*

80. **below:** *The annual meeting and demonstration of the Cornwall County Fire Brigades Union in Coinagehall Street, Helston, in August, 1913. I hope the figure leaping from the roof was a dummy. RIC Photo, Helston 7.*

81 & 82. ***above and below:*** *Floods have been an all too regular occurrence in Cornwall. Boscastle was hit by torrents which claimed one life in 1958.*

STORM OF DEATH

Snatched by the cruel sea

Hurricane force winds and mountainous waves claimed the lives of 16 people on the Cornish coast. Eight lifeboatmen died in a courageous second attempt to rescue the crew of a stricken coaster.

The Penlee lifeboat, launched from the village of Mousehole on Saturday night had already braved 40ft waves to pluck four people to safety from the coaster Union Star.

Rescue organisations believe the lifeboatmen turned back in a courageous but ill-fated attempt to save the four others.

It will be a bleak Christmas for many families. Twelve children lost their fathers in the disaster. It is thought that the lifeboat may have been holed and sunk while trying to effect the second part of the rescue.

The director of the Royal National Lifeboat Institution, Rear Admiral Wilfred Graham, said the lifeboat had been "smashed to smithereens".

He added: "I have never seen a big boat like that smashed in the way this boat clearly was. The vessel was dashed against the rocks and smashed into pieces."

By last night the bodies of six people had been recovered, and the grim search continued for the remaining ten. There were five crewmen, one women and two children on the 1,400 ton Dublin-registered merchant ship.

Beat on the side

Last night, almost 24 hours later, the coaster remained upside down aground on rocks, 350 yards west of Tater-dhu Light near Lamorna.

Royal Navy divers from HMS Drake worked in appalling conditions.

THE VICTIMS

Coxswain of the Penlee lifeboat was Charlie Trevelyan Richards, 56, a bachelor who was well-respected in the village. The other lifeboatmen were: "Stephen Madron, 35, the mechanic, who was married with two children; Nigel Brockman, 43, married with three children; Barry Torrie, 33, married with two children.

Kevin Smith, 23, was single, like 22-year-old Gary Wallis.

John Blewett, 43, had two children, and Charles Greenhaugh, 46, whose body was the first to be found, had three daughters. He was licensee at the village's Ship Inn.

Six of the eight people aboard the Union Star had been named last night.

The captain was Henry Morton, 33, of Witham, Essex. With him was his South African wife Dawn, 34, and her two daughters by a previous marriage, Sharon Brown (16) and Dinah (14).

The ship's mate was named as James Whittaker, 34, of Queenborough, Kent, and the other British crewman was George Sedgewick, 44, of Hull.

The names of the other two crew members, both Portuguese, were not available.

said: "I was amazed when I heard the lifeboat had managed to pick up four the first time."

Commander George Cooper, deputy chief of operations for the RNLI said: "By the amount of wreckage, it is obvious that the lifeboat came into contact with something."

Mr Mike Sutherland, Penlee's deputy launching officer, said: "No radio message was received from the lifeboat and no distress flares fired. Whatever happened that day

lifeboatmen just for the hell of it. He knows very well that one day the chips may be down, and this sort of thing is going to happen. "The sea is very cruel, utterly relentless, and there are times when it may overcome the most stalwart hearts — and that is what it has done on this occasion.

"The bravery and the service that is exhibited by lifeboatmen is a beacon for anyone in the country to follow."

Festive lights out in village of grief

GROUPS SHARE SORROW IN THE STREETS

Mousehole was a community sealed off in its private grief yesterday. As police stopped all those without a real purpose from driving along the clifftop road from Newlyn into the village, small groups gathered in the tiny streets and harbour area to talk in disbelief of the tragedy.

In one terrible night, an instant response to other people in distress took the lives of eight brave men and left 12 children fatherless, and widows, parents and friends to grieve. The people of Mousehole, a village where life revolves around fishing and the sea, looked out at the ocean as the huge waves of the night before subsided yesterday.

Helicopters searching for bodies, together with neighbouring lifeboats, could be seen in the distance. Small groups stood around, stunned by the tragedy. The previous night, many of the men had responded to the distress call, but only the full crew of eight could make the fateful trip.

Many of the families listened on their short-wave radios to the conversations between the boats, Coastguards, helicopter and the lifeboat involved in the Union Star rescue attempt.

Worry

Some began to worry when the lifeboat lost radio contact at about 10.30 pm and the helicopter crews eventually came on with their call, which went on for half an hour, saying: "Penlee Lifeboat, if you can hear me, send up one flare."

No flare went up and the search continued. At least at that stage there was some hope, as relatives and friends phoned each other

Knowing the sea as they do, no one in Mousehole held out any real hope that anyone would have survived the 50ft waves in seas which were the worst they had ever seen.

"Mousehole is like us all. We are completely stunned and disbelieving," said Mr. Johnson yesterday. "The village is in a desperate mood at the moment, grief-stricken."

Mousehole's seasonal celebrations are usually second to none. The Christmas lights in the harbour are famous, a colourful tradition enjoyed by people from all over Cornwall who go to see them, and join in the quayside carol services. They have survived storms before to stay bright over the Christmas period, but last night the lights of Mousehole were switched off as the season of festivity came to a cruel end.

Tradition

For many people in the Mousehole area, the lifeboat is a family tradition. Second coxswain and mechanic Stephen Madron, lifeboat, but will try to be in the crew as soon as he is 17.

"This just makes me want to do it even more," said Baden yesterday. "Those men tried to save someone else's life and they died for it. If ever I'm sitting at home and the maroons go off, I'll run."

Roll Call

The final roll call of lost lifeboatmen was:

Coxswain Trevelyan Richards, 56, unmarried, who lived with his widowed mother in Mousehole. He served 30 years with the Penlee Lifeboat, eleven of them as coxswain.

In 1975 he was awarded the RNLI Bronze Medal for gallantry for his part in the attempt to rescue the crew of the coaster Lovat.

He also received a letter of commendation later for saving a Belgian trawler from rocks off Newlyn. He was presented to the Queen, with the crew, on the Saturday's trip. he was a fish salesman.

Crewman Charles Greenhaugh, 46, married with three daughters, was landlord of the Ship Inn at Mousehole. He was previously landlord of the Mount View Hotel at Long Rock, near Penzance.

Emergency mechanic John Blewett, 43, married with two children, was a British Telecom engineer. He was associated with many Mousehole organisations.

Crewman Kevin Smith, 23, leaves a mother, younger brother and sister. He joined the crew in 1975.

Crewman Barrie Torrie, 33, leaves a wife and two small sons. A fisherman, he had been a lifeboat crew member for 15 years.

Crewman Gary Wallis, 22, lived in Mousehole with his father, mother and sister. He was a fisherman who joined the lifeboat crew in 1979.

Awards

Stephen Madron, Nigel Brockman, Barry Torrie and Kevin Smith were awarded a medal service certificate for their part in the attempt to rescue the crew of the Lovat in 1975. None of the crew survived.

The Bishop of Truro, the Rt Rev. Peter Mumford, did what he could to comfort the bereaved families when, with the vicar of Paul, the Rev. Hugh Cadman, he visited Mousehole yesterday morning.

They called at a number of homes in the village.

83 & 84. ***opposite page and above:*** *The Penlee lifeboat disaster, five days before Christmas 1981, when eight lifeboatmen died as they took the Solomon Browne literally onto the deck of the Union Star to take off her crew, the captain's wife and her two children. The tragedy followed two previous occasions when lifeboatmen lost their lives in an attempt to save others. The St Ives lifeboat overturned with the loss of six of her crew when she put out to help a stricken steamer in January, 1939. The Padstow lifeboat, James Steven No 4, capsized with the loss of three lives while helping a ketch in April, 1900.*

DAY OCTOBER 21

MAN ENGINE BREAKS

FOUR MEN KILLED AT LEVANT MINE

OTHERS ENTOMBED

Not since the flooding of Wheal Owens in 1893 has so disastrous a mining accident taken place in the St Just district as occurred at Levant Mine yesterday.

Through the breaking of the man engine, when the men were ascending, it was known last night at 9 o' clock that four men had been killed and there were some men still in the mine with injuries.

The roll call had not been made last night, and the bodies had not been brought to the surface, so it was impossible to say definitely who the victims are. A few men with minor injuries had come up before 8 o' clock and had gone to their homes. It was also ascertained that a few men were isolated underground through the damage done to the shaft, but they are alive and have been spoken to. Organized parties were hastily constructing ladderways to enable them to get out, the permanent ladderway in that part of the shaft having been carried away by the crash.

MEN NOT HEARD OF

The manager of the mine said last evening that there were six or seven men not yet heard of, but he hoped they would be got up before this morning.

The scene of the accident was the main engine shaft, the engine which has historic interest as being the only man engine in use in the mines of the world. It has been continuously used in Levant for perhaps 70 years. It works to 300 fathoms deep, on a big wood rod, and it is propelled up and down by a 12-foot stroke. Attached to the rod at every 12 feet is a platform which accommodates a man, and corresponding with this is a platform at every 12 feet on the side of the shaft. As the rod ascends or descends the man steps off from the platform to the corresponding stationery platform and so eventually reaches his destination by six lifts. When being used to its fullest extent the man engine accommodates 150 men, and it was whilst it was being used by the men coming up that the accident happened, the afternoon shift having gone down the mine by the same method. It was thought by the management that 100 to 120 men were on the engine at the time.

OCTOBER 22, 1919

MINE CALAMITY

OVER 30 DEATHS AT LEVANT

WORK OF RESCUE

9 BODIES BROUGHT TO SURFACE

In its extent and horror the accident which happened at Levant Mine on Monday afternoon has far exceeded any realization which was formed of it up to a late hour the same night.

Though several men had not been accounted for, it was scarcely believed that the worst had happened. Yesterday brought the disaster into a clearer perspective, and by last night fears were entertained that the death roll was a heavy one. It was not officially ascertainable how many men had lost their lives; they could not tell, they said, until the bodies had been discovered amongst the debris and brought up.

Resources were utilized to rescue the living. Up to last evening nine bodies had been brought up, and of these eight were identified as follows:-

Peter Branwell, married, aged about 58, St Just.

Thos Branwell (his brother), married, aged about 60, Carnyorth.

John T Augwin, married, aged between 50 and 60, St Just.

Sampson Osborne, single, aged between 40 and 50, St Just.

Wm H Tregear, married, aged between 50 and 60, St Just.

Matthew Newton, married, aged 60, St Just.

Wm E Waters, single, aged about 25, St Just.

Hy Andrews, married, aged about 46, St Just.

Besides these, one which is badly mangled, is unidentified and a man who was brought up alive has since died at his home at St Just. His name is:-

Stephen J Brewer, single, aged 19, St Just.

When found he was badly crushed and suffering severe shock. Pinned down by debris, he had to remain until rescued and taken out at 4 o'clock yesterday morning — eleven hours after the accident. With six rescued alive there were 21 unaccounted for last evening.

LEVANT DISASTER

INQUEST OPENED ON 18 VICTIMS

12 STILL MISSING

KING'S MESSAGE OF SYMPATHY

St Just, Pendeen, Trewellard, and Boscaswell combined are so small that you cannot find them on many maps, yet they house a whole world of woe within their greyness. Today the Levant Mine is the axis of their world, around which all their thoughts revolve, above which their laments hover, and to which every ear is inclined. These four small Cornish villages have borne the brunt of the disaster, and it is their townsfolk who are bereaved. They are very quiet and silent, wrapped in a gloomier aspect than ever before. In many houses simple love and cheerfulness have been transformed by a twirl of fate's kaleidoscope into desolation and despair, and the downdrawn blinds bear mute testimony to the grief which they conceal. The very loungers at the street corners have an unwonted quietness, and their conversation is subdued, so that the sharp clatter of feet on the flinty roads seems as though it were a sacrilege against the stillness.

Today the miner might strut as though the splendorous panoply of a Paladin were his. What does it matter though his trousers are earth-stained and ragged, and his coat is torn and shabby? In the eyes of his fellows he is a hero, radiant with the romance of his heroism. Not for nothing has he undergone the peril of the valley of the shadow and braved its unknown terrors, or ventured into a Gethsemane of appalling evil on a perilous quest of mercy. To him belongs the distinction of those who have been tried, and have not been found lacking. Yet because of the immensity of the fear which even brave men apprehend, and because of the sights that met his affrighted gaze, the miner is awed into taciturnity. Question him as to his exploits, ask him about the disaster which engulfed so many of his comrades, but do not expect satisfaction. He was ready to give.

85. Some cuttings from The Western Morning News coverage at the time.

86. **above:** *Levant Mine, near St Just-in-Penwith. Mining is a dangerous occupation. The worst tragedy in Cornwall was the Levant Disaster of October, 1919, when the main engine shaft which took men underground and lifted them to the surface broke and swept away everything in the upper part of the shaft.*

87. **below:** *Firemen, with hoses like snakes, pump out a flooded Penryn in 1953.*

88. ***above:*** *After all those disasters here is a miraculous escape. A Hawker Hunter jetplane crashed on Tintagel in July, 1979. It went across a field just missing a man up a ladder, and ended up wedged between two houses.*

89. ***below:*** *The jet finished a few feet from a petrol tanker and filling station owner Jack Cann.*

RAGING TORRENT FLINGS CARS ASIDE LIKE TOYS

MAN DROWNS AS FLOOD HORROR HITS POLPERRO

One man was swept out to sea and drowned last night and others were rescued after being trapped as flood water up to 10ft high rushed through the Cornish fishing village of Polperro. Streams running through the village, which lies in a steep valley, burst their banks and poured mud, debris, and water through the streets. Emergency vehicles trying to reach the scene found their paths blocked by high flood water.

The missing man was named as 81-year-old Mr Wilfred Haycock. He was swept away from a window of the Mill House Hotel, which is beside the River Pol, as he grasped for a lifeline thrown to him by would-be rescuers. His body was later recovered from the harbour.

Mr Haycock was the senior partner in the Mill House Hotel family business. He lived at the hotel with his son-in-law and daughter, Mr and Mrs Ted Sendall.

Eye witnesses said a wall of water swept through the village, flinging cars aside like toys. It flooded houses,

band has run the Polperro Garage for 40 years.

"It was like the sort of disaster you see on television happening

90. Polperro suffered on September 24th, 1976, a night I remember as I was acting as chief sub-editor. When the enormity of what was happening in Polperro began to come through I had to recall production staff who had gone and we brought this edition out at about 3.00 am in the morning.

TANKER OIL: MINISTER ARRIVES FOR FIGHT TO SAVE BEACHES

18-mile patch moving from Scillies towards mainland

NAVY BRINGS SPECIAL CHEMICALS

As a vast patch of oil spread out from the crippled Liberian tanker Torrey Canyon off the Isles of Scilly last night, the Prime Minister sent Mr Maurice Foley, Under-Secretary for Defence (Navy), to lead the battle to save Cornish beaches. He flew to Plymouth to co-ordinate oil dispersal plans.

Three Navy ships, the Clarbeston, Barrosa, and the tug Sea Giant, were carrying hundreds of gallons of special chemicals to use on the oil patch, now said to be 18 miles long and two miles wide, moving east towards the Cornish coast. The tanker has lost about a quarter of her 120,000-ton cargo since she ran aground on the Seven Stones reef on Saturday.

HELICOPTER LIFT

All but four of her crew of 36 Italians were taken off yesterday. Nine were winched up by helicopter and flown to St. Mary's, Isles of Scilly, and the rest were being taken to Penzance aboard the Trinity House vessel Stella, after being transferred from a lifeboat.

The nine who were taken off by helicopter had declined to jump from the tanker into the St. Mary's lifeboat after one of the men fell into the sea. He was quickly rescued.

The captain remained on board with three officers and two salvage men from the Dutch tug Utrecht. An attempt to re-float the tanker failed yesterday after a line which the Utrecht managed to get aboard parted almost immediately.

Another attempt to haul the vessel off the rocks will be made this morning.

BIGGEST THREAT TO SEASON

The tanker Torrey Canyon (61,263 tons), pouring thousands of tons of crude oil into the sea, represents the biggest threat to the Cornish seaside holiday season the county has ever known.

Bound from the Persian Gulf to Milford Haven and carrying 120,000 tons of oil, the tanker struck the reef at about 8.30 on Saturday morning. The rocks tore holes the length of her starboard side, breaking open ten of her 18 oil tanks, and instantly their evil smelling contents spread over the sea.

Capt. J Summerlee, who piloted the B.E.A. passenger helicopter from Penzance to the Isles of Scilly over the scene only a few minutes after the accident, said that even then he could smell the oil from three miles downwind

Ald. Mumford and Mr R Phillips, Clerk, to Plymouth from St. Mary's.

Mr Sidney Grieve, Clerk to West Penwith Rural Council, said that as soon as they heard of the matter the Medical Officer and the Health Officer did their utmost to get the Government departments concerned to realise the magnitude and seriousness of the threat to the Cornish beaches.

"If this oil lands anywhere here, either in the Isles of Scilly or on the West Penwith beaches, or up the coast, it is going to be a terrific task to get rid of it," he declared.

Mr Peter Tonks, Deputy Mayor of St. Ives, said: "The horribleness of it is that we are so helpless. We know this great patch of oil is out there, but we don't know where it is going to strike.

TANKER BLAZES AS NAVY PLANES STRIKE

RAF adds petrol mixture to keep fire burning

But then sea dowses flames

Eight Royal Navy Buccaneers flew down from the North of Scotland yesterday and dropped 40,000lbs of high explosives on to the wreck of the 61,000-ton tanker Torrey Canyon, sending smoke 3,000ft into the air and setting the sea of oil around her alight. The aircraft swept in singly at 2,500ft and about 30 out of 40 bombs scored direct hits on the two visible sections of the ship.

In the second wave of the Government's plan to keep the area ablaze and prevent more oil from fouling West-country beaches, 26 RAF Hunter jets from Chivenor (North Devon) dropped auxiliary fuel tanks containing paraffin and petrol, which added to the flames.

At dusk last night only the aft part of Torrey Canyon was visible above the heavy seas, but despite a further bombing raid by two Buccaneers the blaze was extinguished by the high tide.

An Admiralty spokesman said last night in Plymouth that a fleet of Hunters had so far dropped 5,200 gallons of aviation fuel on the blazing slick which was half a mile in radius. The aircraft were swooping in at five-minute intervals after refuelling at St. Mawgan.

"The strike has been a success," said the spokesman. "The tanker is ablaze from stem to stern and the slick is spreading slowly south-west.

91 & 92. ***opposite page and above:*** *We became aware of the dangers of major oil pollution from supertankers when the Torrey Canyon ran aground on the Seven Stones reef in March, 1967.*

93. ***above:*** *Air raid damage in October, 1940. Believed to be Padstow.*

94. ***above:*** *Boys hunting shrapnel after an air raid at Padstow, 1940.*

95. ***above:*** *Evacuees arriving in Cornwall.*

Cornwall at War

Restrictions and lack of film meant few photographs were taken by civilians of wartime Cornwall. However, at the beginning and end of the war pictures were taken by our staff and others of the way the civilians, and those service people stationed here, viewed Hitler's threat.

*96. **above:** Air Training Corps cadets learning Morse Code at St Austell.*

*97. **below:** Fire bomb practice at Lostwithiel, May, 1941.*

98, 99 & 100. ***below:*** *Air raid damage in Falmouth.*

*101. **below:** Children taking part in a gas mask drill at the Mickey Mouse Club in a St Austell cinema.*

*102. **above:** Indian Army troops parade through St Austell.*

103. **above:** *A clear message from the Spitfire Fund at Wadebridge.*

104. **above:** *Evacuees learning to ride at Lanhydrock House.*

105. **above:** *Evacuees on a children's outing at St Columb in 1940.*

106. **below:** *War Weapons Week at Fowey.*

107. **above:** *Emergency fire appliances parading through Fowey during War Weapons Week.*

108. **below:** *More fire engines.*

109. ***above:*** *All hands to the pump. A woman training with the Fire Guard at St Austell.*

110. ***above:*** *Stirrup pump and hose practice at St Austell.*

*111. **above:** Patrol boats on the Fal.*

*112. **above:** Crantock Girls School, Newquay, on a book salvage drive in January, 1944.*

*113. **above:** The Fire Girls on parade in Salute the Soldier Week at Lostwithiel in May, 1944.*

114. ***above:*** *The Home Guard on parade in Liskeard.*

115. ***above:*** *Community feeding at Camborne.*

116. ***above:*** *World boxing champion Joe Louis meets the troops at Bodmin, May, 1944.*

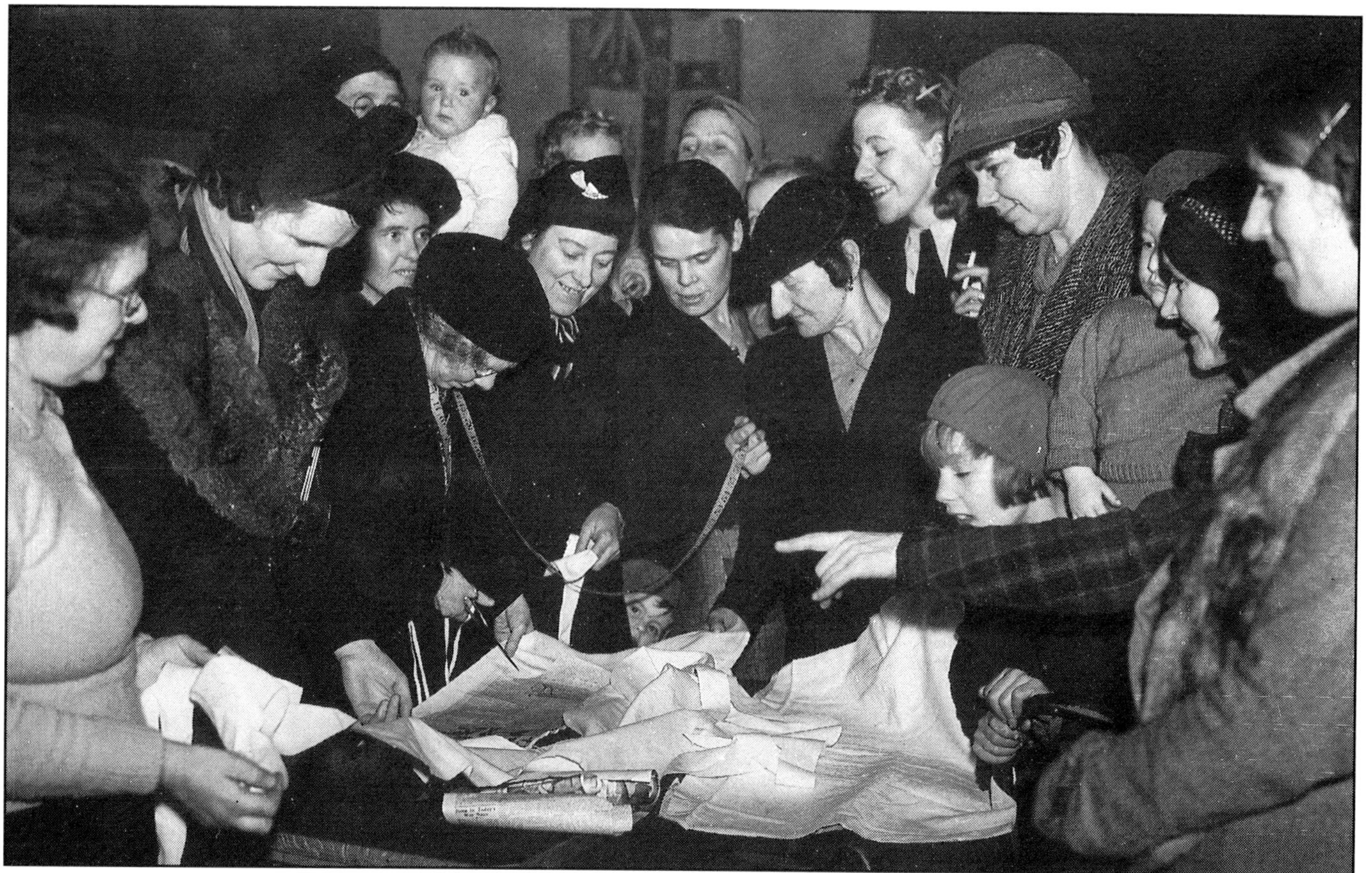

117. ***above:*** *Folk putting out clothes at the St Austell Evacuee Centre.*

118. ***below:*** *The GIs meet the "Obby Oss" at Padstow, May Day, 1944.*

119. ***above:*** *Another shot of May Day in Padstow, 1944.*

120. ***below:*** *Montgomery meets Prince Berhard of the Netherlands on a Cornish airfield.*

121. ***above:*** *Blow me, the war's over. Bugle Band march through their village on VE Day.*

122. ***below:*** *VE day in Cornwall, August 10th, 1945.*

Cornwall in Colour

123 & 124. **above and below:** *Truro old and new. Picture 123 shows one of Truro's oldest buildings, the Old Mansion House. Built in 1709, it was the home of Samuel Enys, a wealthy merchant. After falling into disrepair it has now been restored by a firm of solicitors. Picture 124 shows the most modern major building in Truro and Cornwall, the new Courts of Justice, which has won a number of architectural awards.*

125. Falmouth Docks attract work from the world's shipping. Here is the oil tanker BP Energy undergoing work in the dry dock.

126. "Aren't they steep," wrote the sender of this 1906 postcard showing the steps at Jacob's Ladder, Falmouth.

127. Godrevy lighthouse, on an island near Gwithian, before the First World War.

128. *Pendennis Castle, Falmouth, which is worth a visit today.*

129. ***above:*** *A spot much loved by Truro residents, where the only difference between the 1905 scene and today is that there are now more boats moored up. The message on the back of the card reads: "This is our steamer. We came in it from Falmouth. So I got the carpets at Gills and they are sending it by the omnibus on Saturday."*

130. ***below:*** *Shows Sunny Corner today.*

131. The Old Abbey House at Padstow.

132. **above:** *Ships in Falmouth Bay, rather different from the tankers, ferries, oil rigs and pleasure craft seen today.*

133. **below:** *Truro Cathedral, built in the 1880s, towers above the shop roofs in the centre of the city.*

134. Exploring the Cavern at Land's End at the turn of the century.

135. Heanton Terrace, Redruth, with two very smartly dressed little girls.

136. Landing fish at St Ives.

137. ***above:*** *Cornwall led the way in being the first county to have an air ambulance to get patients to hospital in the shortest possible time. Here is the air ambulance taking off to go to an emergency during the celebrations of its third birthday at Newquay in April, 1990.*

138. ***below:*** *The late Donald Healey, a Cornishman who had a remarkably inventive life, pictured with two of his creations, a 1956 Austin-Healey 100 and a 1946 Healey 2.4 litre Westland Roadster. His son, Bic Healey, tells me that in 1972 he bought the Roadster on behalf of an American collector for £325. Earlier this year it was on sale at £125,000.*

139. An archway in the Digey, St Ives.

140. **above:** *Callington Fore Street in 1906.*

141. **below:** *Calstock Fore Street in 1913.*

142. **above**: *Back Road, St Ives.*

143. **below:** *The road leading down to Bodinnick Ferry, which takes vehicles and foot passengers across to Fowey.*

144. Fore Street, Millbrook.

145. Old Cornish fish sellers.

*146. **above:** At work. Harvesting at St Day in 1932.*

*147. **above:** At play. Hurling at St Columb in 1990.*

*148. **above:** Work and play. Fishing and pleasure boats off Flushing, near Falmouth.*

*149. **above:** The Old Men's Dance at a Port Isaac concert in May, 1944.*

*150. **below:** Two hundred Cornish miners, with their lights aglow, greet King George VI at Camborne School of Mines.*

151 & 152. **above and below:** *Women were working in the Cornish mines at the turn of the century. These pictures at Dolcoath Mine, Camborne, show the Bal Maidens with the Overseer, Mine Captain and other workers.*

153. **above:** *Skiffle was the rage in the late 1950s. Here is the Truro Scout Skiffle Band in 1959.*

154. ***above:*** *The Padstow "Obby Oss", 1963.*

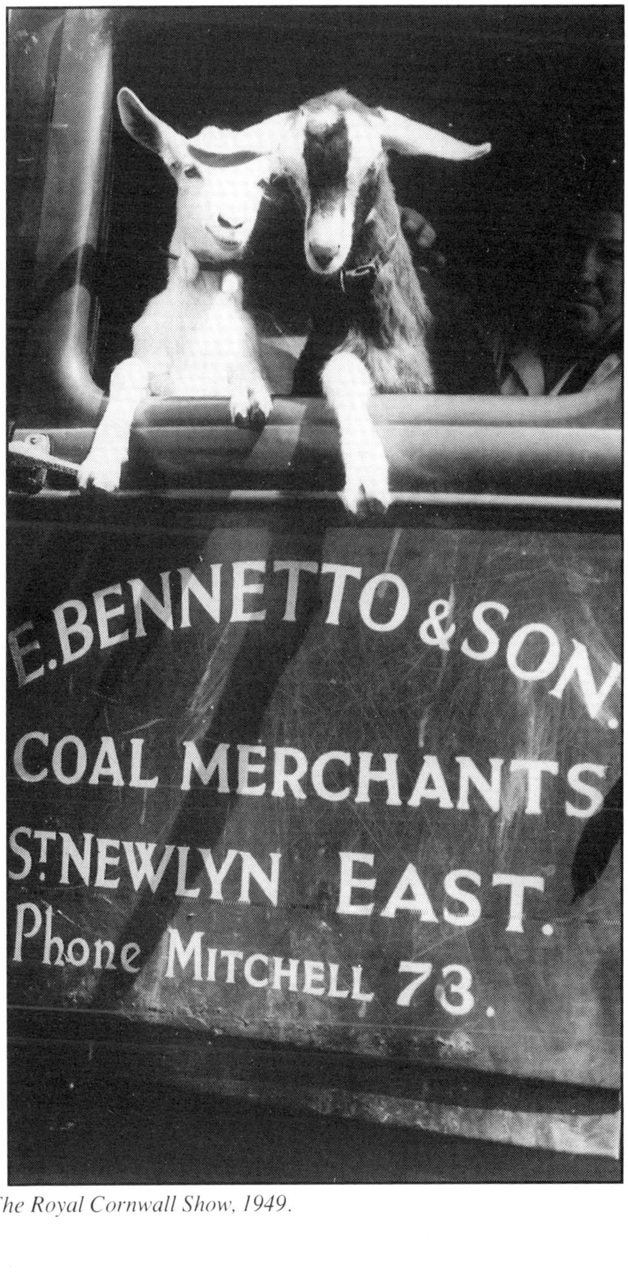

155 & 156. ***above left and above right:*** *The Royal Cornwall Show, 1949.*

157. ***above:*** *Discussing the potato crisis in Truro in the 1950s.*

158. ***below:*** *Plymouth Cycle Club at Portwrinkle in 1898. RIC Photo, Sheviock 1.*

159. **above:** *Fishermen and others posed by a pilot gig at Trevellas, St Agnes, around 1900. RIC Photo, St Agnes TV 1.*

160. **below:** *Drilling contest above the harbour at Trevaunance Cove, St Agnes, on Regatta Day, 1910. PC Beney is seeing fair play. RIC Photo, St Agnes P3.*

161. **above:** *St Austell Volunteer Band, 1907. RIC Photo, St Austell P1.*

162. **below:** *Quarry men at Dannon Chapel, St Teath, with my great grandfather centre.*

163. ***above:*** *Model yachts carried in procession through Newquay for a regatta on the Gannel, around 1910. RIC Photo, F13.*

164. ***below:*** *A postman at St Agnes delivering a letter to Tom Benney, the Town Crier and bill-poster. RIC Photo, St Agnes P5.*

165. **above:** *Flora Day, 1910, in Coinage Hall Street, Helston. Because of the death of Edward VII on May 7th, Flora Day was postponed until July. RIC, Helston 27.*

166. **below:** *Furry Dance at Higher Pengwedna, Helston, May 3rd, 1904. RIC, Helston 18.*

167. ***above:*** *Bostock and Woomwell's Circus in procession outside the Great Western Hotel at Newquay in the early 1900s. RIC, Newquay, F3.*

168. ***below:*** *J C Burrow and Herbert Hughes on a photographic excursion in 1913. The party is relaxing at the end of Bude Breakwater. RIC, Bude 38.*

169. **above:** *Painting boats at Port Isaac.*

170. **above:** *Support from the church, in the shape of the Bishop of Truro, the Rt Rev Peter Mumford, and Mrs Mumford, during the tin crisis of 1986.*

*171. **above:** Folk dancing at an annual event which drew schoolchildren to Newquay each year. This is 1952.*

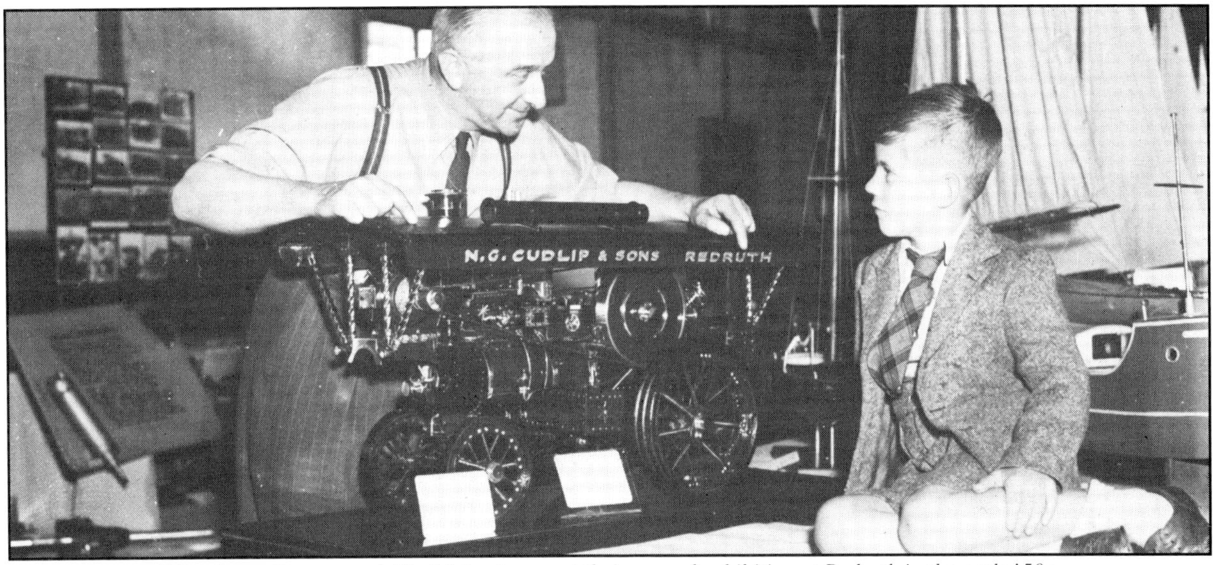

*172. **above:** Perranporth Model Engineers at their annual exhibition at Redruth in the early '50s.*

*173. **above:** Beach cricket at Perranporth around 1950.*

174. **above:** *The Cornwall rugby team's front row of Richard Keast, Graham Dawe and John May, which took them to Twickenham in 1989, battle it out with Middlesex in the 15-15 draw at Redruth which meant the end of their county championship final ambitions in 1990. This and the following photographs from the semi-final at Redruth on March 3rd, 1990, are by The Western Morning News Chief Photographer John Chapman.*

175. **above:** *Cornwall second row Andy Reed in expansive mood. Martin Haag is in front of him and Jon Polglass behind.*

176. **above:** *The Cornwall rugby selectors at a nail-biting moment at Redruth. Coach David Thomas has his head in his hands, but "Bonzo" Johns and Don Palmer are more philosophical.*

177. ***above:*** *The Chief Guide, Lady Baden Powell, visits Truro in 1950.*

178 & 179. ***above and below:*** *The Falmouth Marine Band, who kept Cornwall's spirits going with their "music" at the county championship games.*

180. What sweeter way to end a look at Cornwall at work and play than John Chapman's study from the Callington Honey Fair.

People and Places

181. Prince Charles and Princess Diana, the Duke and Duchess of Cornwall, at St Columb Major in May, 1983, their first official visit to Cornwall following their wedding.

182. ***above:*** *Look closely, you could be in this picture if you were at the Lanivet baby show in May, 1944.*

183. ***below:*** *The Countess Mountbatten inspecting the St John Ambulance at Newquay in 1944.*

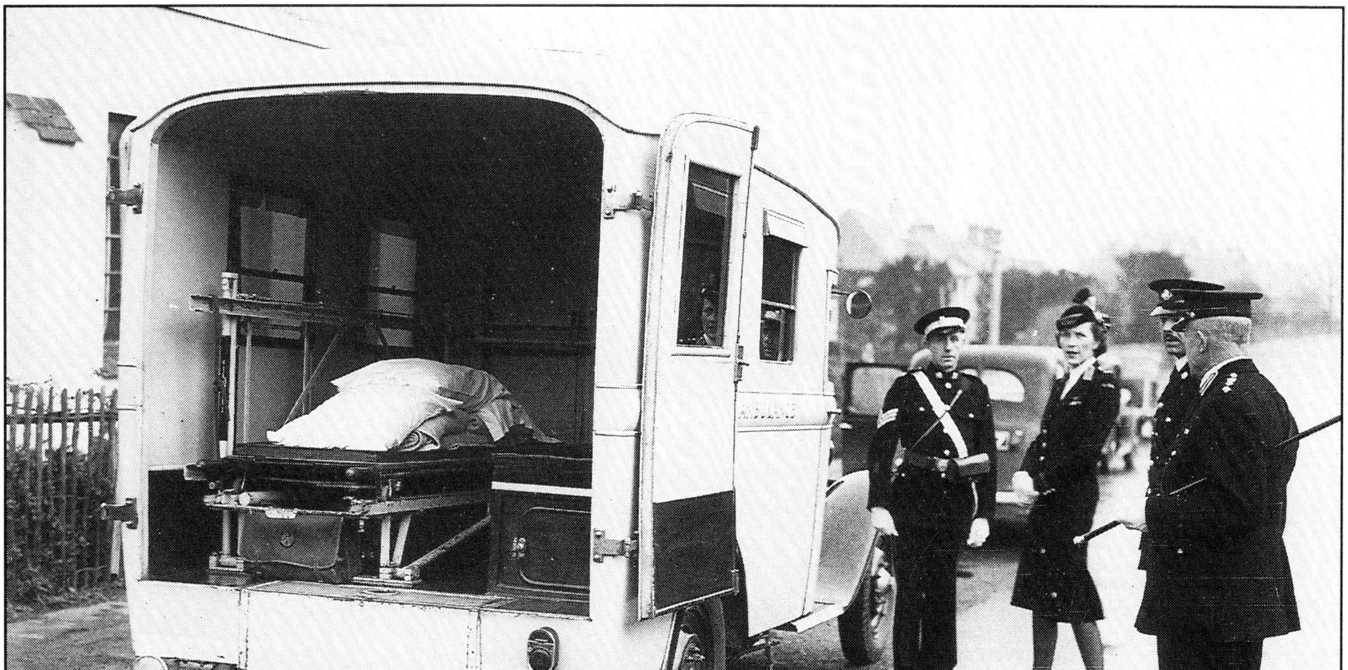

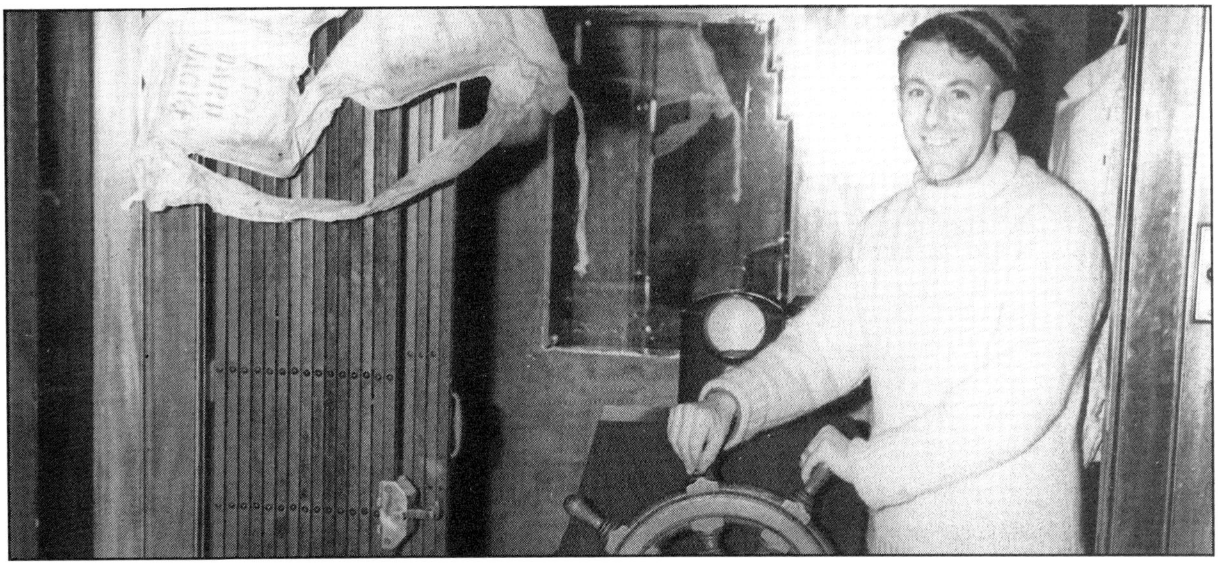

184 & 185. ***above and below:*** *Cornwall has been a popular venue for cinema and television filming. In the late 1940s the people of Mevagissey had a brief taste of stardom for the filming of "Johnny Frenchman" with Pat Roc and Tom Walls. Fisherman Herbert Thomas became a local celebrity.*

186. ***below:*** *Novelist Dame Daphne du Maurier at her desk, which is now on display at the pub which one of her most popular stories, "Jamaica Inn", made famous.*

187 & 188. **above left and above right:** *The television series "Poldark" showed Cornwall to the world. Here the author, Winston Graham, who spent his youth at Perranporth, watches filming while Ross Poldark (Robin Ellis) and Demelza (Angharad Rees) have a chat outside St Winnow Church.*

189 & 190. **above left and above right:** *"Penmarric" was another popular series filmed both in and about a Cornish family. Here are Annabelle Leventon, who played the heroine Janna Roslyn, and Ralph Bates, a Cornishman who appeared in both this series and Poldark.*

191. ***above:*** *David Penhaligon, the Truro MP who became known as the Voice of Cornwall before his death in a car crash, always had plenty of work on his desk — but he had time to read The Western Morning News as well.*

192. ***above:*** *Two sisters who spent so long in Cornwall they almost became old friends. The tankers Methane Princess and Methane Progress were laid up in the Fal because of a glut in world shipping.*

193. ***above:*** *The Lugger Inn at Fowey in the 1890s. RIC Photo, Fowey 98.*

194 & 195. ***below left and below right:*** *French Onion Johnnies at Penryn just after the war had plenty of eager customers.*

196. **above:** *Camelford at the turn of the century.*

197. **above:** *The opening of the Camborne sewage tunnel from Bell Lake to North Cliffs in the 1920s.*

198. **below:** *Motorists and children at the old pack horse bridge at St Thomas, Launceston, a scene which thankfully has not changed too much over the years.*

199. ***above:*** *A posed postcard extolled the virtues of Newquay in the early 1900s.*

200. ***above:*** *Hawker's Vicarage at Morwenstow, with its Gothic chimneys in the form of miniature church towers.*

201. ***below:*** *St Just-in-Penwith in the 1920s.*

202 & 203. **above and below:** *The Foots, a distinguished Cornish family at their home at Pencrebar, Callington, in February, 1960. As well as Sir Isaac Foot, the former Liberal MP for Bodmin, are sons who became Leader of the Labour Party, Solicitor General, Governor of Cyprus and members of the House of Lords.*

204 & 205. **above and below:** *Cornwall has always had a close association with the Royal family. Here the Prince of Wales arrives to open the pier named after him at Falmouth in May, 1905. RIC Photos, PWP 2 and 8.*

206. **above:** *The Duke of Windsor often visited Cornwall in the 1930s. Here he is seen watching men at work at Trenance Lake, Newquay. The caption of the time said: "The Prince of Wales has taken a keen interest in the problems of the unemployed, watching men at work constructing a lake in Trenance Gardens. Rather than be idle they are giving their services voluntarily."*

207. **below:** *He also visited the Duchy Oyster Farm at Port Navas on the River Helford.*

208. *After the Duke's abdication the new King visited Cornwall. At Liskeard with the Duchy Land Steward, T M Stanier, the rousing reception from schoolchildren brought a smile to his face.*

209. ***above:*** *At a ceremony in the Castle Green at Launceston in 1937 the King received the feudal dues from his loyal Cornish subjects.*

210. ***below:*** *After the war the King and Queen visited a china clay tip near St Austell, escorted by Lord Aberconway.*

211 & 212. **above and top, overleaf:** *The Queen Mother still visits Cornwall, and took a great interest in the county's agriculture at the Royal Cornwall Show in 1985.*

213. ***below:*** *Do you remember the craze for walking from John o' Groats to Land's End in the early 1960s? Here Dr Barbara Moore strides through Launceston, and there are many faces I recognise among those there to greet her.*

214 & 215. ***above and below:*** *Wendy Lewis won £1,000 offered by Billy Butlin for her walk from John o' Groats in 1960, and most of West Penwith was there to cheer her.*

216 & 217. **above and below:** *Fresh faced beauty in the 1950s and early '60s. Falmouth's Flower Queen for 1954 and Miss Cornwall senior and junior in 1960.*

218. **above:** *Folk dancing at Camborne in the '50s.*

219. **above:** *Mother Goose arrives for a pantomime in Redruth around 1950.*

220. The now-pedestrianised street scene is not too different today.

221. ***above:*** *St Petroc's Church, Bodmin, around 1900.*

222. ***below:*** *The winding gear used for unloading ships at Trevaunance harbour around 1900.*

223. **above:** *Donald Healey, a Cornishman who was a motoring legend throughout the world, was born at Perranporth when it was a tiny village. He opened a garage at Perranporth where he built both cars and radios. In 1931 he won the Monte Carlo rally, and three years later he moved to the Midlands as a director of the Triumph Motor Company. Later he designed the famous Healey series of sports cars. He is pictured at Perranporth in 1935 with the Triumph Straight 8 Dolomite which he designed.*

224. **below:** *Charles Causley, the distinguished poet, was born at Launceston and still lives there. He is a Queen's Gold Medallist for poetry, a Doctor of Letters and a CBE, but I remember him best as an inspiring teacher when I was a pupil at the National School at Launceston, where he taught for 25 years. The photograph is by James Lyne.*

100 Years On

225 & 226. **above and below:** *We started in the 1890s with the Great Blizzard, and the dawn of the 1990s showed us we are still at the mercy of the elements. These two pictures by David Brenchley, of Cornish Photonews, show the force of the storms which hit the county as they swept waves over Porthleven in December 1989.*

227. The storm of January 25th, 1990, ripped up Cornwall's magnificent trees, especially at Mount Edgcumbe. Our picture shows Maker Church.

228 & 229. ***above and below:*** *These pictures by David Brenchley's colleague Colin Higgs show the first wreck of the 1990s. Picture 228 is of the Toledo at Pendower Beach, with the tug Simson. Picture 229 below shows the MV Cecil Japan which was wrecked on a howling night at Deadman's Cove, near Hell's Mouth. A helicopter from RNAS Culdrose rescued all but one of the crew in atrocious conditions.*

230. Progress marches on, but it still takes a skilled man like David Dawson to repair a weathercock at St Minver by climbing up a ladder, the same as in the last century. Picture by John Lyne.

231 & 232. **above and below:** *Old and new exist side by side in Cornwall. The old brewery at the Blue Anchor, Helston, continues to please its customers while the Devenish Brewery at Redruth does things on a bigger and more modern scale. Happily the beer tastes good from both.*

233. The new tunnel beneath Saltash sees the people of that area, here with their MP Robert Hicks, stepping out into the light.

234 & 235. **above left and above right:** *Cornwall ranges from scenes like the old lanes and shops near the People's Palace at Truro to the space age "listening station" near Bude.*

236. **below:** *The release of a swan rescued by the RSPCA, pictured by John Lyne, gives us the opportunity to see the links from Cornwall to Plymouth, the Tamar Bridge, opened in 1963, and Brunel's Victorian railway bridge of 1859.*

237. Cornwall's future depends on her children and her schools. Our last picture shows the Princess of Wales at the village school at Kea, near Truro, in March 1990.